Our Family History

HOW TO TRACE YOUR FAMILY TREE

with Janet Reakes

BayBooks
An imprint of HarperCollins*Publishers*

A BAY BOOKS PUBLICATION
An imprint of HarperCollinsPublishers

First published in Australia in 1983
CollinsAngus&Robertson Publishers Pty Limited
Reprinted 1983, 1984, 1985, 1986, 1987 (twice), 1989
This edition revised in 1992 by Bay Books, of
CollinsAngus&Robertson Publishers Pty Limited (ACN 009 913 517)
A division of HarperCollinsPublishers (Australia) Pty Limited
25 Ryde Road, Pymble NSW 2073, Australia

HarperCollinsPublishers (New Zealand) Limited
31 View Road, Glenfield, Auckland 10, New Zealand

HarperCollinsPublishers Limited
77-85 Fulham Palace Road, London W6 8JB, United Kingdom

Copyright © Bay Books 1992

This book is copyright.
Apart from any fair dealing for the purposes of private study,
research, criticism or review, as permitted under the Copyright
Act, no part may be reproduced by any process without written
permission. Inquiries should be addressed to the publisher.

National Library of Australia
ISBN 1 86378 029 7

Special thanks to Betty Burcham
for supplying the photographs in this book
and to Donna Hay for the cover photograph

Cover background photographed by Quentin Bacon
with styling by Donna Hay

Printed in Hong Kong

5 4 3 2 1
96 95 94 93 92

Contents

Husband's Genealogy 6
Wife's Genealogy 7
Our Children 8
Our Grandchildren and Descendants 9
Our Family Tree 12
Husband's Personal File 18
Husband's Personal History 19
Husband's Family 20
Husband's Parent's Family 22
Husband's Grandparents — Father's Side 26
Husband's Grandparents — Mother's Side 30
Husband's Great-Grandparents 34
Wife's Personal File 38
Wife's Personal History 39
Wife's Family 40
Wife's Parent's Family 42
Wife's Grandparents — Father's Side 46
Wife's Grandparents — Mother's Side 50
Wife's Great-Grandparents 54
Our Family's Origins and Immigration Record 58
Our Homes 60
Where Our Ancestors Lived 62
Schools, Teachers and Graduations 64
Important School Achievements 66
Clubs and Organisations 68
Our Family's Employment Record 70
Family Pets 72
Family Cars and Other Vehicles 74
Favourite Things 76
Heirlooms and Collections 78
Favourite Family Hobbies 80
Favourite Family Sports 81
Treasured Memories of Our Children 82
Special Occasions 84
How to Trace Your Family Tree 88
Useful Addresses 93

This Record was Compiled by

_____

and

Was Started on

_____

This is to Record That

_____

and

_____

Were United in Marriage

Place of Ceremony _____

City or Town _____

State _____

Date _____

Married by _____

Witnesses _____

_____

_____

_____

Husband's Genealogy

Husband's Full Name _____

Date of Birth _____

Place of Birth _____

Father's Full Name _____

Mother's Full Name _____

Brothers and Sisters _____

_____

_____

_____

_____

Wife's Genealogy

Wife's Full Name _____

Date of Birth _____

Place of Birth _____

Father's Full Name _____

Mother's Full Name _____

Brothers and Sisters _____

_____

_____

_____

_____

Our Children

Full Name _____

Date of Birth _____ Place of Birth _____

Full Name _____

Date of Birth _____ Place of Birth _____

Full Name _____

Date of Birth _____ Place of Birth _____

Full Name _____

Date of Birth _____ Place of Birth _____

Full Name _____

Date of Birth _____ Place of Birth _____

Full Name _____

Date of Birth _____ Place of Birth _____

Our Grandchildren and Descendants

Photographs

Photographs of your children and grandchildren.

Our Family Tree

PLACE FAMILY
PHOTOGRAPH HERE

Husband's Full Name _____

Wife's Full Name _____

Date of Marriage _____

Place of Marriage _____

Our Children _____

_____

_____

_____

_____

_____

Husband's Paternal Grandfather's Name

Husband's Paternal Grandmother's Name

Date of Marriage   Place of Marriage

Children

Husband's Father's Name

Husband's Mother's Name

Date of Marriage   Place of Marriage

Children

Husband's Maternal Grandfather's Name

Husband's Maternal Grandmother's Name

Date of Marriage   Place of Marriage

Children

Wife's Paternal Grandfather's Name

Wife's Paternal Grandmother's Name

Date of Marriage   Place of Marriage

Children

Wife's Father's Name

Wife's Mother's Name

Date of Marriage   Place of Marriage

Children

Wife's Maternal Grandfather's Name

Wife's Maternal Grandmother's Name

Date of Marriage   Place of Marriage

Children

		Husband's Great-Great-Grandfather
Husband's Great-Grandfather		Husband's Great-Great-Grandmother
Husband's Great-Grandmother		Husband's Great-Great-Grandfather
		Husband's Great-Great-Grandmother
		Husband's Great-Great-Grandfather
Husband's Great-Grandfather		Husband's Great-Great-Grandmother
Husband's Great-Grandmother		Husband's Great-Great-Grandfather
		Husband's Great-Great-Grandmother
		Husband's Great-Great-Grandfather
Husband's Great-Grandfather		Husband's Great-Great-Grandmother
Husband's Great-Grandmother		Husband's Great-Great-Grandfather
		Husband's Great-Great-Grandmother
		Husband's Great-Great-Grandfather
Husband's Great-Grandfather		Husband's Great-Great-Grandmother
Husband's Great-Grandmother		Husband's Great-Great-Grandfather
		Husband's Great-Great-Grandmother

Great-Great-Great-Grandparents

Mr & Mrs   Née

Mr & Mrs   Née

Mr & Mrs   Née

Mr & Mrs   Née

Mr & Mrs   Née

Mr & Mrs   Née

Mr & Mrs   Née

Mr & Mrs   Née

Mr & Mrs   Née

Mr & Mrs   Née

Mr & Mrs   Née

Mr & Mrs   Née

Mr & Mrs   Née

Mr & Mrs   Née

Mr & Mrs   Née

Mr & Mrs   Née

Wife's Great-Great-Grandparents

Wife's Great-Grandfather

Wife's Great-Grandmother

Wife's Great-Great-Grandfather

Wife's Great-Great-Grandmother

Wife's Great-Great-Grandfather

Wife's Great-Great-Grandmother

Wife's Great-Grandfather

Wife's Great-Grandmother

Wife's Great-Great-Grandfather

Wife's Great-Great-Grandmother

Wife's Great-Great-Grandfather

Wife's Great-Great-Grandmother

Wife's Great-Grandfather

Wife's Great-Grandmother

Wife's Great-Great-Grandfather

Wife's Great-Great-Grandmother

Wife's Great-Great-Grandfather

Wife's Great-Great-Grandmother

Wife's Great-Grandfather

Wife's Great-Grandmother

Wife's Great-Great-Grandfather

Wife's Great-Great-Grandmother

Wife's Great-Great-Grandfather

Wife's Great-Great-Grandmother

Great-Great-Great-Grandparents

Mr & Mrs	Née
Mr & Mrs	Née
Mr & Mrs	Née
Mr & Mrs	Née
Mr & Mrs	Née
Mr & Mrs	Née
Mr & Mrs	Née
Mr & Mrs	Née
Mr & Mrs	Née
Mr & Mrs	Née
Mr & Mrs	Née
Mr & Mrs	Née
Mr & Mrs	Née
Mr & Mrs	Née
Mr & Mrs	Née
Mr & Mrs	Née

Husband's Personal File

PLACE HUSBAND'S
PHOTOGRAPH HERE

Husband's Full Name _____

Date of Birth _____ Place of Birth _____

Occupation _____

Special Interests _____

_____

Personal Achievements _____

_____

_____

Date of Death _____ Place of Burial _____

Remembered by his friends and relatives for _____

_____

_____

_____

_____

Husband's Personal History

This brief biography should include highlights of the husband's life, education, attainments, work, travels and the events which gave him the greatest joy or satisfaction.

Husband's Family

On this page, fill in the particulars of the husband's brothers and sisters, together with their children (his nephews and nieces).

Name _____

Born _____ Died _____ Spouse _____

Children _____

Name _____

Born _____ Died _____ Spouse _____

Children _____

Name _____

Born _____ Died _____ Spouse _____

Children _____

Name _____

Born _____ Died _____ Spouse _____

Children _____

Name _____

Born _____ Died _____ Spouse _____

Children _____

Name _____

Born _____ Died _____ Spouse _____

Children _____

This space is for recording the personal histories of the husband's family, whose names appear on the opposite page. Write here your special memories of your brothers and sisters and share them with your descendants.

Husband's Parents' Family

Fill in the particulars of the husband's father, his brothers and sisters (husband's uncles and aunts) and the latter's children (husband's cousins).

Name _____

Born _____ Died _____ Spouse _____

Children _____

Name _____

Born _____ Died _____ Spouse _____

Children _____

Name _____

Born _____ Died _____ Spouse _____

Children _____

Name _____

Born _____ Died _____ Spouse _____

Children _____

Name _____

Born _____ Died _____ Spouse _____

Children _____

Name _____

Born _____ Died _____ Spouse _____

Children _____

Personal anecdotes and special memories of those named on the opposite page.

Husband's Parents' Family
Continued

Fill in the particulars of the husband's mother, her brothers and sisters (husband's uncles and aunts) and the latter's children (husband's cousins).

Name _____

Born _____ Died _____ Spouse _____

Children _____

Name _____

Born _____ Died _____ Spouse _____

Children _____

Name _____

Born _____ Died _____ Spouse _____

Children _____

Name _____

Born _____ Died _____ Spouse _____

Children _____

Name _____

Born _____ Died _____ Spouse _____

Children _____

Name _____

Born _____ Died _____ Spouse _____

Children _____

Personal anecdotes and special memories of those named on the opposite page.

Husband's Grandparents - Father's Side

Fill in the particulars of the husband's grandfather, his brothers and sisters (husband's great uncles and aunts) and the latter's children.

Name _____

Born _____ Died _____ Spouse _____

Children _____

Name _____

Born _____ Died _____ Spouse _____

Children _____

Name _____

Born _____ Died _____ Spouse _____

Children _____

Name _____

Born _____ Died _____ Spouse _____

Children _____

Name _____

Born _____ Died _____ Spouse _____

Children _____

Name _____

Born _____ Died _____ Spouse _____

Children _____

*Personal anecdotes about those named on the opposite page.
What historical times did they live through?*

Husband's Grandparents - Father's Side
Continued

Fill in the particulars of the husband's grandmother, her brothers and sisters (husband's great uncles and aunts) and the latter's children.

Name _____

Born _____ Died _____ Spouse _____

Children _____

Name _____

Born _____ Died _____ Spouse _____

Children _____

Name _____

Born _____ Died _____ Spouse _____

Children _____

Name _____

Born _____ Died _____ Spouse _____

Children _____

Name _____

Born _____ Died _____ Spouse _____

Children _____

Name _____

Born _____ Died _____ Spouse _____

Children _____

Personal anecdotes about those named on the opposite page.
What historical times did they live through?

Husband's Grandparents – Mother's Side

Fill in the particulars of the husband's grandfather, his brothers and sisters (husband's great uncles and aunts) and the latter's children.

Name _____

Born _____ Died _____ Spouse _____

Children _____

Name _____

Born _____ Died _____ Spouse _____

Children _____

Name _____

Born _____ Died _____ Spouse _____

Children _____

Name _____

Born _____ Died _____ Spouse _____

Children _____

Name _____

Born _____ Died _____ Spouse _____

Children _____

Name _____

Born _____ Died _____ Spouse _____

Children _____

*Personal anecdotes about those named on the opposite page.
What historical times did they live through?*

Husband's Grandparents - Mother's Side
Continued

Fill in the particulars of the husband's grandmother, her brothers and sisters (husband's great uncles and aunts) and the latter's children.

Name _____

Born _____ Died _____ Spouse _____

Children _____

Name _____

Born _____ Died _____ Spouse _____

Children _____

Name _____

Born _____ Died _____ Spouse _____

Children _____

Name _____

Born _____ Died _____ Spouse _____

Children _____

Name _____

Born _____ Died _____ Spouse _____

Children _____

Name _____

Born _____ Died _____ Spouse _____

Children _____

Personal anecdotes about those named on the opposite page.
What historical times did they live through?

Husband's Great-Grandparents

Name _____

Born _____ Died _____ Spouse _____

Children _____

Name _____

Born _____ Died _____ Spouse _____

Children _____

Name _____

Born _____ Died _____ Spouse _____

Children _____

Name _____

Born _____ Died _____ Spouse _____

Children _____

Name _____

Born _____ Died _____ Spouse _____

Children _____

Name _____

Born _____ Died _____ Spouse _____

Children _____

Name _____

Born _____ Died _____ Spouse _____

Children _____

Name _____

Born _____ Died _____ Spouse _____

Children _____

Personal anecdotes about those named on the opposite page.
What historical times did they live through?

Photographs

Photographs of the husband and his relatives.

Wife's Personal File

Wife's Full Name _____ Née _____

Date of Birth _____ Place of Birth _____

Occupation _____

Special Interests _____

_____

Personal Achievements _____

_____

_____

Date of Death _____ Place of Burial _____

Remembered by her friends and family for _____

_____

_____

_____

_____

Wife's Personal History

This brief biography should include highlights of the wife's life, education, attainments, work, travels and the events which gave her the greatest joy or satisfaction.

Wife's Family

On this page, fill in the particulars of the wife's brothers and sisters, together with their children (her nephews and nieces).

Name _____

Born _____ Died _____ Spouse _____

Children _____

Name _____

Born _____ Died _____ Spouse _____

Children _____

Name _____

Born _____ Died _____ Spouse _____

Children _____

Name _____

Born _____ Died _____ Spouse _____

Children _____

Name _____

Born _____ Died _____ Spouse _____

Children _____

Name _____

Born _____ Died _____ Spouse _____

Children _____

This space is for recording the personal histories of the wife's family, whose names appear on the opposite page. Write here your special memories of your brothers and sisters and share them with your descendants.

Wife's Parents' Family

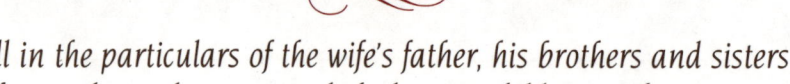

Fill in the particulars of the wife's father, his brothers and sisters (wife's uncles and aunts) and the latter's children (wife's cousins).

Name _____

Born _____ Died _____ Spouse _____

Children _____

Name _____

Born _____ Died _____ Spouse _____

Children _____

Name _____

Born _____ Died _____ Spouse _____

Children _____

Name _____

Born _____ Died _____ Spouse _____

Children _____

Name _____

Born _____ Died _____ Spouse _____

Children _____

Name _____

Born _____ Died _____ Spouse _____

Children _____

Personal anecdotes and special memories of those named on the opposite page.

Wife's Parents' Family
Continued

Fill in the particulars of the wife's mother, her brothers and sisters (wife's uncles and aunts) and the latter's children (wife's cousins).

Name _____

Born _____ Died _____ Spouse _____

Children _____

Name _____

Born _____ Died _____ Spouse _____

Children _____

Name _____

Born _____ Died _____ Spouse _____

Children _____

Name _____

Born _____ Died _____ Spouse _____

Children _____

Name _____

Born _____ Died _____ Spouse _____

Children _____

Name _____

Born _____ Died _____ Spouse _____

Children _____

Personal anecdotes and special memories of those named on the opposite page.

Wife's Grandparents – Father's Side

Fill in the particulars of the wife's grandfather, his brothers and sisters (wife's great uncles and aunts) and the latter's children.

Name _____

Born _____ Died _____ Spouse _____

Children _____

Name _____

Born _____ Died _____ Spouse _____

Children _____

Name _____

Born _____ Died _____ Spouse _____

Children _____

Name _____

Born _____ Died _____ Spouse _____

Children _____

Name _____

Born _____ Died _____ Spouse _____

Children _____

Name _____

Born _____ Died _____ Spouse _____

Children _____

Personal anecdotes about those named on the opposite page.
What historical times did they live through?

Wife's Grandparents - Father's Side
Continued

Fill in the particulars of the wife's grandmother, her brothers and sisters (wife's great uncles and aunts) and the latter's children.

Name _____

Born _____ Died _____ Spouse _____

Children _____

Name _____

Born _____ Died _____ Spouse _____

Children _____

Name _____

Born _____ Died _____ Spouse _____

Children _____

Name _____

Born _____ Died _____ Spouse _____

Children _____

Name _____

Born _____ Died _____ Spouse _____

Children _____

Name _____

Born _____ Died _____ Spouse _____

Children _____

*Personal anecdotes about those named on the opposite page.
What historical times did they live through?*

Wife's Grandparents - Mother's Side

Fill in the particulars of the wife's grandfather, his brothers and sisters (wife's great uncles and aunts) and the latter's children.

Name _____

Born _____ Died _____ Spouse _____

Children _____

Name _____

Born _____ Died _____ Spouse _____

Children _____

Name _____

Born _____ Died _____ Spouse _____

Children _____

Name _____

Born _____ Died _____ Spouse _____

Children _____

Name _____

Born _____ Died _____ Spouse _____

Children _____

Name _____

Born _____ Died _____ Spouse _____

Children _____

*Personal anecdotes about those named on the opposite page.
What historical times did they live through?*

Wife's Grandparents - Mother's Side
Continued

Fill in the particulars of the wife's grandmother, her brothers and sisters (wife's great uncles and aunts) and the latter's children.

Name ———————————————————————————————

Born ——————— Died ——————— Spouse ———————————————

Children ——————————————————————————————

Name ———————————————————————————————

Born ——————— Died ——————— Spouse ———————————————

Children ——————————————————————————————

Name ———————————————————————————————

Born ——————— Died ——————— Spouse ———————————————

Children ——————————————————————————————

Name ———————————————————————————————

Born ——————— Died ——————— Spouse ———————————————

Children ——————————————————————————————

Name ———————————————————————————————

Born ——————— Died ——————— Spouse ———————————————

Children ——————————————————————————————

Name ———————————————————————————————

Born ——————— Died ——————— Spouse ———————————————

Children ——————————————————————————————

*Personal anecdotes about those named on the opposite page.
What historical times did they live through?*

Wife's Great-Grandparents

Name _____

Born _____ Died _____ Spouse _____

Children _____

Name _____

Born _____ Died _____ Spouse _____

Children _____

Name _____

Born _____ Died _____ Spouse _____

Children _____

Name _____

Born _____ Died _____ Spouse _____

Children _____

Name _____

Born _____ Died _____ Spouse _____

Children _____

Name _____

Born _____ Died _____ Spouse _____

Children _____

Name _____

Born _____ Died _____ Spouse _____

Children _____

Name _____

Born _____ Died _____ Spouse _____

Children _____

*Personal anecdotes about those named on the opposite page.
What historical times did they live through?*

Photographs

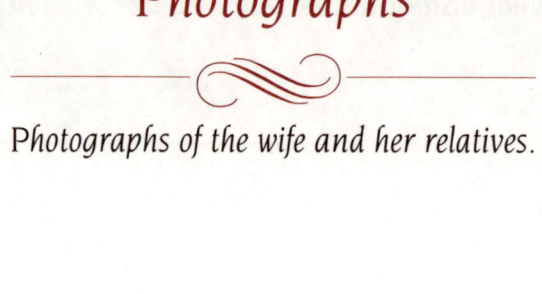

Photographs of the wife and her relatives.

Our Family's Origins and Immigration Record

ONE-NAME SOCIETIES

An interesting development in family history during recent years is the study and collection of information relating to particular surnames. As a result, One-Name Societies have sprung up in the United Kingdom, North America and Australasia. Your state genealogical society can tell you whether your family name is represented among these One-Name Societies and, if so, where to contact the appropriate society.

Our Homes

Street Address _____

City or Town _____ State _____

Date of Purchase or Lease _____

Resided from _____ To _____

Recollections _____

_____

_____

_____

_____

Street Address _____

City or Town _____ State _____

Date of Purchase or Lease _____

Resided from _____ To _____

Recollections _____

_____

_____

_____

Street Address _____

City or Town _____ State _____

Date of Purchase or Lease _____

Resided from _____ To _____

Recollections _____

_____

_____

_____

_____

Use this space for photographs of your homes.

Where Our Ancestors Lived

Use this page for photographs of your ancestors' homes.

Schools, Teachers and Graduations

Use this page for photographs of graduations and other memorable school events.

Important School Achievements

This page is for recording important awards, events and amusing anecdotes from your school days.

Use this page for photographs of events recorded on the opposite page.

Clubs and Organisations

Use this page for photographs of club outings and members.

Our Family's Employment Record

Where we worked and positions achieved

Family Pets

*Just recalling the names of family pets will bring back
a flood of happy memories.*

Use this page for photographs of favourite family pets.

Family Cars and Other Vehicles

When did your family acquire its first car? As you try to recall all the motor vehicles owned by family members you will doubtless find yourself enjoying the nostalgia of those days.

Owner	Make/Model/Year	Colour	Dates of Ownership

Owner	Make/Model/Year	Colour	Dates of Ownership

Favourite Things

Husband's and wife's
songs, records, books, clothing, possessions,
entertainments, recipes, food, drinks, places

Children's
songs, records, toys, clothing, stories, games, places

Heirlooms and Collections

Describe all the family heirlooms, identifying their original owners and how the articles were passed down through successive generations. Also list any special collections made by family members, indicating, if possible, why and when they began collecting.

Favourite Family Hobbies

Favourite Family Sports

Treasured Memories of Our Children

Special Occasions

Anniversaries, weddings, religious events, stories

Photographs

Photographs of treasured memories and special events.

How to Trace Your Family Tree

Janet Reakes

If you enjoy jigsaw puzzles, crosswords, detective stories and the thrill of a chase, you'll love genealogy!

The hardest part of genealogy — (or tracing the family tree) is making the decision to start. Once you've started the rest is easy — well, almost!

Genealogy (pronounced 'jeanie–allergy') is a contagious disease, once you've started you can't stop. That's why it's called an allergy.
Here are a few general hints on how to trace your family tree.

1 Get a black fine point pen, and a pencil. Write all your details in black pen but pencil in any unconfirmed information. Get a folder and some copy safe, acid free, clear plastic sleeves to file your certificates and other documents.

2 When writing information on the pedigree charts always enter the name as it is said, i.e. Janet Elizabeth Reakes and not Reakes, Janet Elizabeth. This is because some names are both Christian names and surnames, i.e. Thomas Martin which in reverse is Martin Thomas. All women should be entered in under their *maiden* name and not married name. For example, my mother was born Margaret Berry, her married name is Reakes. She is not recorded as Margaret Reakes nee Berry, but just Margaret Berry. If a nickname is used put William Henry (known as Harry) Reakes, or if there is a surname change put it as Robert Lane alias Matthews.

3 All dates should be recorded in full. Abbreviations of months such as Sep for September is acceptable but not full numerical dates such as 3/4/50. To Australians this means the 3rd of April, to Americans it reads March the 4th. Historically the calendar changed in 1752 and up until that year the first month was March (September was the seventh month, October the eighth month etc — hence their names). Therefore, if this date 3/4/50 referred to the year 1750 it would mean the 3rd of June — as June was the 4th month of the old year. (See my book A *to Z of Genealogy* under L for Lady Day for full details.)

4 Interview everyone in the family. Don't procrastinate! The problem when you start tracing the family tree is that people die, and they are always the ones you should have asked. We all wish we'd listened to grandma! Interview using cassette tape or video if possible. Otherwise take a shorthand course if you are taking notes, in order to keep up with the stories. Remember, if the family won't tell you anything, they are hiding something, and the more they won't say the more you want to find out what it is, so persevere until you do. And don't forget you're not there to judge but to record the facts!
A favourite quote I like to use is this:

> *If you could see your ancestors, all standing in a row*
> *Would you be proud of them, or don't you really know?*
> *Some strange discoveries are made in climbing family trees*
> *But some of them perhaps do not particularly please*
> *If you could see your ancestors all standing in a row*
> *There might be some of them, perhaps, you wouldn't care to know*
> *But there's another question which requires a different view*
> *If you could meet your ancestors would they be proud of you?*

5 Search the cemeteries to copy out inscriptions on family headstones. Many cemeteries have been indexed and published in print, microfilm and microfiche format. These can be viewed at major libraries and genealogical centres.

6 When you have collected all the family documents, bibles and photos from your relatives, and visited the family graves, it's time to build upon the framework you have made by purchasing additional certificates where necessary.

Australia

Before buying certificates you should consult the indexes to the civil registration records, some of which are on public access. These indexes will allow you to find the correct entry number, and by quoting this in the states of Victoria and New South Wales, you can obtain cheaper copies.

Most indexes can be found in state libraries, major council libraries, LDS (Latter-day Saints) Family History Libraries and also Genealogy Society libraries. Individuals may also purchase them.

Indexes publicly available at present are:

New South Wales: births, deaths and marriages 1856 to 1905

Queensland: births 1859 to 1904; marriages and deaths 1859 to 1914 (Note: Queensland was New South Wales before 1859.)

Victoria: births 1853 to 1913; marriages 1853 to 1930 and deaths 1853 to 1960

South Australia: births, deaths and marriages 1841 to 1907

Western Australia: births, deaths and marriages 1842 to 1905

Tasmania: births, deaths and marriages 1838 to 1899 (also the complete certificates)

Northern Territory: births, deaths and marriages 1870 to 1902

Before these dates there are church records, and although the indexes to church records date back to the First Fleet, the information recorded on the documents is not as detailed as government certificates issued after the above dates. Indexes are also available for early church records in each state.

• Information found on certificates is more detailed for New South Wales, Victoria and Queensland.

Birth Certificate: typical information includes name of child, birth date and place, sex, parents' names, father's occupation, parents' ages and birth places, their marriage date and place and previous issue, witnesses to the birth and informant. (In Queensland, you must ask for the marriage details to be included when ordering a birth certificate since 1890.) In South Australia, Western Australia and Tasmania the early certificates only gave name of child, birth date and place, sex and parents' names. Western Australia improved its certificates in 1896 when the extra information was added. South Australian certificates were improved in 1907 and Tasmania in 1896 and again in 1902. Northern Territory certificates improved in 1908 to give parental details.

Marriage Certificates: typical New South Wales, Victoria and Queensland Marriage Certificate information includes date and place of marriage, names of both parties, their ages, birth places, residences, fathers' names, occupations, and mothers' names and witnesses. Early certificates in the other states did not give birth places of the bride and groom, nor parental details.

Tasmanian certificates include this after 1896; South Australia added the names of the fathers of the bride and groom in 1856, but it took until 1964 for the mothers' names to be included. Birth places of bride and groom were not added until 1908. Western Australian certificates include birth places of the couple after 1923 and mothers' names after 1896. Northern Territory certificates did not improve until 1949, although birth place was added after 1928.

Death Certificates: typical New South Wales Victoria and Queensland Death Certificate information includes: name of deceased and place of death, cause of death, parents' names, informant, place buried, religion and witnesses, where married, what age and whom to; birth place and length of residence in the colony (if born overseas) and children of deceased.

Birth place was not recorded on Tasmanian certificates until 1897 and parents' names and number of issue not until 1914. Western Australia improved its certificate information in 1896 and South Australia in 1907. However, South Australian death certificates still do not give parents' names and marital details.

• If your ancestor was born overseas, he or she had to come here by ship. Shipping records are kept at the Archives Office of whatever state the person arrived. There are several types of shipping records:

i) *Assisted Passenger lists*: normally indexed, and easy to search. These include people whom the government selected to bring over as emigrants. They normally come from the British Isles, although there are some from Germany. The Immigration Board Records for NSW Immigrants in the early days were very detailed with information such as the names of each passenger's parents, whether they were alive or dead, and if alive where living. Also listed are relatives in the colony. Records for the other states are not as good as the NSW Immigration Board Lists. Nevertheless, most researchers want to know what ship their original ancestor came over on.

ii) *Unassisted Passenger lists*: usually unindexed and sometimes people are only numbered, not named. If your ancestor came via New Zealand or USA or was well off, then he or she would be amongst these records.

iii) *Convict records*: indexed. Convicts came to NSW from 1788 to 1842, Tasmania from 1803, and Western Australia from 1850 to 1868. Each Archive Office holds the appropriate convict records. The content of them varies over the time period.

iv) *Crew/Military lists*: unindexed. If you fail to find your ancestor coming in on a ship remember to check the other states' records, for example someone may immigrate to Tasmania, not like it and come by coastal vessel to Port Phillip. Also consider spelling problems. Byrnes may be under Burns, Beirnes, O'Byrne or Birn. Spelling of surnames was never rigid and your surname may be spelt many ways. Accents and poor education were the two major causes of name corruptions. A German immigrant may have anglicised his name, i.e. Muller to Miller, Bachaus to Backhouse etc.

• A useful shortcut to research is the Genealogical Research Directory (GRD), which is an annual publication showing who's tracing whom in the family tree. It commenced publication in 1981 and has built up a huge data bank of entries and is 960 pages thick. These directories can be found in major public libraries, genealogy societies and also can be purchased by private individuals. When writing to anyone in the GRD please enclose return postage.

• There are various genealogy societies in Australia and a complete listing of addresses is given on page 93. Most major cities and towns have at least one genealogy group.

• If your ancestors were born overseas you need to find an exact place of origin. As mentioned earlier, birth, death and marriage certificates could provide this information. Shipping records and occasionally gravestones, will record where the person came from.

The Church of Jesus Christ of Latter-day Saints (nicknamed LDS or Mormon Church) has many family history libraries throughout Australia. Through these libraries you can access over two million rolls of microfilms covering every country of the world. Visits to LDS libraries are free, however donations are appreciated towards running costs. To access the rolls of microfilm you need to look up the Family History Library Catalogue (found in the library) which will give you the film number to quote for hire. The fee for hiring a film for a month is approximately $6. The order is sent to the Australian Family History Service Centre in Sydney and a copy is despatched back a few weeks later to the library you visited. You cannot take the films out of the library. Types of records available include parish registers, census records, apprenticeship records, immigration, probates and military records.

LDS libraries in Australia can be found at:
Australian Capital Territory and New South Wales: Canberra, Dapto, Greenwich, Lismore, Mortdale, Newcastle, Orange, Parramatta, Mount Druitt, Taree and Tamworth
Northern Territory: Alice Springs, Darwin
Queensland: Brisbane, Ipswich, Bundaberg, Cairns, Isle of Capri, Hervey Bay, Nambour, Rockhampton, Sunnybank, Townsville, Toowoomba, Gympie, Kingaroy and Mt Isa
South Australia: Marion and Modbury, Port Pirie and Whyalla
Tasmania: Hobart and Launceston
Victoria: Bendigo, Geelong, Mildura, Northcote, Swan Hill, Dandenong, Traralgan, Wangaratta and Wantirna
Western Australia: Attadale, Yokine

• A shortcut to research can be made by consulting the International Genealogical Index, which is an index of over 200 million names worldwide. It is compiled by the Church of Jesus Christ of Latter-day Saints and lists christenings and marriages between the mid 1550s to about 1880. It is not 100 per cent complete, but is a good shortcut, especially for research in the British Isles. Copies of the IGI can be found in major libraries, LDS Family History libraries, genealogy groups and with private researchers.

New Zealand

Europeans

Civil registration of European births, deaths and marriages commenced in 1848 although it did not become compulsory until 1856. The New Zealand Government has released microfiche copies of these indexes up to 1920. They can be found in many libraries, genealogy societies and LDS Family History Centres as well as similar resource centres in Australia. Information on certificates has improved over the years.

Birth Certificates: originally, a birth certificate gave the following information: name, birthdate and birthplace, sex, father's name and occupation, mother's name and maiden name. After 1876 additional information included the age and birthplaces of each parent.

Death Certificates: until 1876 these certificates recorded name of deceased, where and when died, age, sex, usual place of residence, profession or occupation, and cause of death.

After 1876 the information improved to include parents' names, mother's maiden name, father's occupation, name of medical attendant who certified the death, when and where buried, where born and length of residence in New Zealand. Also included are details on whether the deceased was married, where married, age at marriage, spouse's name, age of widow, ages and sex of living issue. It is important to note that additional information is recorded in the original entry that is not typed up on a certificate. For instance, the name of the informant is missing from a birth certificate, and from 1876 the date and place of parents' marriage, and from 1916 the previous issue of the couple.

Therefore when applying for a birth certificate after 1876 it is important to ask for the parents' marriage details to be added. It is also important that you ask for an RG 100 if applying for certified copies of birth.

Extra information on death certificates contained in the original registers includes the informant's name and address, the name of the officiating minister and the religion.

Marriage Certificates: Until 1881 the following information can be found on a New Zealand Marriage Certificate: where and when married, names of bride and groom, conjugal status (bachelor, spinster, widow, widower) and groom's occupation.

After 1881 the birth place and usual residence of each party, their parents' full names including mothers' maiden name and their fathers' occupations were added.

In 1867 the first New Zealand legislation was passed allowing for divorce so this may also be mentioned on a certificate after this year.

Information in the original registers but not on a certificate include the full names, addresses and occupations of the witnesses, the name of the minister and the religious denomination.

When requesting a copy of a marriage after 1880 always ask for an RG 118, otherwise the standard and less informative RG 117 is used. The RG 117 is normally used for pre-1880 entries.

Cheaper certificates can be obtained if you only require a microfilm printout of the original. This is quite satisfactory for genealogical purposes.

If it is possible for you or an agent to visit the Registrar General's Office in Lower Hutt then post 1900 entries can be inspected for a small fee. Inspections are limited to three per day, however out of town or overseas visitors may make an appointment to see up to ten post-1900 entries. To book a session you must write and pay several weeks before your intended visit. An inspection costs approximately $5 per entry.

Australians researching New Zealand ancestry can also apply through the New Zealand Consulate's office.

Maoris

In 1911 the registration of Maori marriages became compulsory. In 1913 Maori birth and death registrations also became compulsory and were kept in separate registers until 1952 when Maori and European marriage entries were combined and in 1961 when births and deaths were combined.

Maori birth entries between 1913 and 1961 also recorded the degree of Maori blood of each parent and the tribe to which they belonged.

Similarly on Maori death certificates, people of more than half Maori blood were registered with the name of their tribe and degree of Maori blood.

The father's occupation was not recorded on a Maori marriage certificate.

Church records contain many Maori christenings, marriages and burials and should be consulted. It is also advisable to first check with your local tribal elder as Maoris kept verbal records of their genealogy. This was important in order to prove ancestral rights to tribal land, enable proper marriages to be conducted and identify relationships within a sub-tribe.

Maori Land Records: the Maori Land Court Minute Books began in 1863 and provide detailed information on Maori families and ownership of tribal lands. They are available at the office of the appropriate Maori Land Courts.

The Department of Maori Affairs has seven Maori Land Districts:

Aotea: District Office, Wanganui
Tairawhiti: District Office, Gisborne
Takitimu: District Office, Hastings
Te Waipounamu: District Office, Christchurch
Tokerau: District Office, Whangarei
Waiariki: District Office, Rotorua
Waikato-Maniapoto: District Office, Hamilton

The minute books are also on microfilm at major public libraries and through the Family History centres of the Church of Jesus Christ of Latter-day Saints (LDS).

Immigration: New Zealand, like Australia, had several ports where immigrant ships could enter. They were Wellington (Port Nicholas), Auckland, Dunedin, Nelson, Lyttleton, Port Chalmers and New Plymouth.

Also, like Australia there is no national index, making searching for ancestors' arrivals a tedious affair unless a port of entry is already known.

Most immigrants would have settled around the vicinity of their port of arrival, so if your ancestors lived near Auckland, then this port would be the first one to check.

The National Archives in Mulgrave Street, Wellington (PO Box 6148 Te Aro, Wellington) has passenger lists for assisted immigrants (pre-1910), but it is not 100% complete.

Unassisted immigrants may have been mentioned as passengers in the newspaper report of the ship's arrival. However, often it will just say 'Thomas Clarke and family, (6)' — indicating his family consisted of six unnamed individuals.

A death certificate issued after 1876 will indicate 'how long in New Zealand' your ancestor had lived.

There is little record kept of trans Tasman arrivals. Your ancestor may have arrived as an assisted immigrant to Australia and then crossed on another ship some time later to New Zealand. This was more common in the latter part of the 1800s and early 1900s.

The New Zealand Society of Genealogists (PO Box 8795 Auckland) also offers a fee paying service for checking immigration records into New Zealand.

So now let the fun begin! Journeying back in the past to find your roots is one of life's greatest adventures. It's a challenging puzzle waiting to be solved, and is fun for all ages. From this hobby will come a fascination for history, literature, geography, detective work, social conditions, correspondence, heritage and hieroglyphics.

And beware, once you've caught the 'gene-allergy bug', you can't be cured.

Remember, you are the most important person in the family tree, write in this book things about yourself to pass down to your descendants. Many of us say with a sigh, "I wish grandma kept her life story, I wish grandma recorded names on the backs of the photos, I wish grandma kept a family bible listing all the births, deaths and marriages".

You're going to be an ancestor yourself one day and they'll say the same things about you. Keep a record of your life, identify photos and note in the bible and this book all the births, deaths and marriages. Your descendants will love you for it.

Good luck and happy hunting!

Janet Reakes
Hervey Bay 1992

Useful Addresses

AUSTRALIA

Registry Offices — (for certificates)

New South Wales:
Registry of Births, Deaths and Marriages
191–199 Thomas Street, Ultimo NSW 2007
(GPO Box 30, Sydney NSW 2001)

Victoria:
Government Statist, 295 Queens Road,
Melbourne VIC 3000
(GPO Box 4332, Melbourne VIC 3001)

Queensland:
Queensland State Archives Office, Compton Road,
Runcorn (for certificates before 1890)

South Australia:
Registrar General, 59 King William Street,
Adelaide SA 5000
(GPO Box 1351, Adelaide SA 5001)

Western Australia:
Registrar General, Oakleigh Building,
22 St Georges Terrace, Perth WA 6000

Northern Territory:
Northern Territory Registrar General, Law Courts
Building, Mitchell Street, Darwin

Tasmania:
Registrar General, GPO Box 541F, Hobart TAS 7001
(for certificates since 1900)

Tasmanian State Archives, 91 Murray Street,
Hobart TAS 7001 (for certificates before 1900)

Australian Capital Territory:
Registrar General, PO Box 1515, Canberra ACT 2601

Archive Offices (for shipping registers, old government records, etc.)

New South Wales:
1 Globe Street, The Rocks, Sydney; also The Kingswood
Repository, O'Connell Street, St Marys (fees charged for
research by correspondence)

Victoria:
Public Record Office, City Search Room, 4th Floor,
318 Little Bourke Street, Melbourne.

Public Record Office, Cherry Lane, Laverton (main
repository, will not research by correspondence)

Queensland:
Compton Road, Runcorn (will not research by
correspondence)

South Australia:
State Library Building, North Terrace, Adelaide

Western Australia:
J.S. Battye Library, 40 James Street, Perth

Northern Territory:
Cary Street, Darwin

Tasmania:
Tasmanian State Archives, 91 Murray Street, Hobart

Genealogical Societies

Capital cities:

New South Wales:
Society of Australian Genealogists, Richmond Villa,
120 Kent Street, Sydney

Victoria:
Genealogical Society of Victoria, 5th Floor, Curtin House,
Swanston Street, Melbourne

The Australian Institute of Genealogical Studies,
PO Box 339, Blackburn VIC 3130

Queensland:
Genealogical Society of Queensland, 1st Floor,
Woolloongabba Post Office, Stanley Street,
Woolloongabba QLD 4102

Queensland Family History Society, PO Box 171,
Indooroopilly QLD 4068

South Australia:
South Australian Genealogy and Heraldry Society,
GPO Box 592, Adelaide SA 5001

Tasmania:
Genealogical Society of Tasmania, PO Box 60,
Prospect TAS 7250

Northern Territory:
Genealogical Society of the Northern Territory,
PO Box 37212, Winnellie NT 5789

Western Australia:
Western Australian Genealogical Society,
Unit 5/48 May Street, Bayswater WA 6053

Australian Capital Territory:
Canberra Heraldry and Genealogical Society,
GPO Box 585, Canberra ACT 2600

Genealogy Societies (Country and Regional)

New South Wales:
Armidale Family History Group, PO Box 1378,
Armidale 2350

Bathurst, Family History Group of, PO Box 1058,
Bathurst 2795

Bega Valley Genealogy Society, PO Box 19, Pambula 2549

Blue Mountains Family History Society, PO Box 97,
Springwood 2776

Botany Bay Family History Society, PO Box 600,
Sutherland 2232

Bourke Family History Group, PO Box 201, Bourke 2840

Broken Hill Family History Group, PO Box 779,
Broken Hill 2880

Burwood-Drummoyne and Districts Family History
Group, c/- Burwood Central Library, 4 Marmaduke Street,
Burwood 2134

Cape Banks Family History Society, PO Box 67,
Maroubra 2035

Casino and District Family History Group, PO Box 586,
Casino 2470

Cessnock Family History Group, PO Box 225, Cessnock 2325

Coffs Harbour District Family History Society, PO Box J42, Coffs Harbour Jetty 2450

Coonamble Family History Group, Glenoria, Gulargambone 2828

Corowa Family History Society, PO Box 104, Corowa 2646

Cowra Family History Group, PO Box 495, Cowra 2794

Deniliquin and District Family History Group, PO Box 144, Deniliquin 2710

Dubbo Macquarie Family History Society, PO Box 868, Dubbo 2830

Eurobodalla Family History Society, PO Box 440, Moruya 2537

Forbes Family History Group, PO Box 574, Forbes 2871

Goulburn and District Family History Society, PO Box 611, Goulburn 2580

Griffith Genealogical and History Society, PO Box 270, Griffith 2680

Gwydir Family History Society, PO Box 61, East Moree 2400

Hastings Valley Family History Group, PO Box 1359, Port Macquarie 2444

Hawkesbury Family History Group, c/- Hawkesbury Library, Dight Street, Windsor 2756

Hornsby Kuring-gai Family History Society, PO Box 500, Turramurra 2074

Hurstville Family Research Group, c/- Hurstville Library, MacMahon Street, Hurstville 2220

Illawarra Family History Group, PO Box 1652, Wollongong 2500

Leeton Family History Society, PO Box 475, Leeton 2705

Lithgow and District Family History Society, PO Box 516, Lithgow 2790

Little Forest Family History Group, PO Box 87, Milton 2538

Liverpool and District Family History Society, PO Box 830, Liverpool 2170

Manning Wallamba Family History Society, PO Box 48, Taree 2430

Milton Ulladulla Genealogical Society, Woodburn Road, via Milton 2538

Moruya and District Historical Society, PO Box 259, Moruya 2537

Nepean Family History Society, PO Box 81, Emu Plains 2750

Newcastle Family History Society, PO Box 189, Adamstown 2289

Orange Family History Group, PO Box 930, Orange 2800

Picton and District History and Family History Society, PO Box 64, Picton 2571

Richmond Tweed Family History Society, PO Box 817, Ballina 2478

Shoalhaven Genealogical Society, PO Box 591, Nowra 2541

Singleton Family History Society, PO Box 422, Singleton 2330

Tamworth and District Family History Group, PO Box 1188, Tamworth 2340

Tumut Family History Group, PO Box 2338, Tumut 2720

Wagga Wagga Family History Society, PO Box 307, Wagga 2650

Wyong Family History Group, PO Box 103, Toukley 2263

Young and District Family History Group, PO Box 586, Young 2594

Queensland:

Caboolture Ancestral Research Group, PO Box 837, Caboolture 4510

Cairns and District Family History Society, PO Box 5069, M80, Cairns 4870

Charters Towers Family History Society, PO Box 783, Charters Towers 4820

Gladstone Family History Society, PO Box 1778, Gladstone 4680

Gold Coast and Albert Genealogical Society, PO Box 2763, Southport 4215

Gympie Ancestral Research Society, PO Box 767, Gympie 4570

Ipswich Genealogical Society, PO Box 323, Ipswich 4305

Mackay Genealogical Society, PO Box 882, Mackay 4740

Maryborough and District Family History Society, PO Box 408, Maryborough 4650

Mount Isa Family History Society, PO Box 1832, Mount Isa 4825

Moura Family History Group, PO Box 145, Moura 4718

Redcliffe and District Family History Group, PO Box 3122, MDC, Clontarf 4019

Central Queensland Family History Association, PO Box 6000, Rockhampton Mail Centre 4702

Townsville Family History Association, PO Box 577, Hermit Park 4812

South Australia:

South East Family History Group, PO Box 758, Millicent 5280

Tasmania:

(Branches of the Genealogical Society of Tasmania):

PO Box 748, Burnie 7320

PO Box 117, Hounville 7109

PO Box 587, Devonport 7310

PO Box 1290, Launceston 7250

Victoria:

Australian Family Researchers, PO Box 52, West Rosebud 3940

Cobram Genealogical Group, PO Box 75, Cobram 3643

Narre Warren and District Family History Group, PO Box 149, Naree Warren 3805

Sale and District Family History Group, PO Box 773, Sale 3850

Swan Hill Genealogical Society, PO Box 1232, Swan Hill 3585

Wimmera Association for Genealogy, PO Box 880, Horsham 3400

Western Australia:

Geraldton Family History Society, c/- 89 Carson Terrace, Geraldton 6530

(Branches of the Western Australia Genealogical Society):

26 Matilda Avenue, Australind 6230

92 Ogden Street, Collie 6225

PO Box 477, Esperance 6450

PO Box 410, Kalgoorlie 6430

Great Southern Branch, PO Box 291, Katanning 6317

PO Box 1091, Mandurah 6210

South West Branch, PO Box 670, Busselton 6280

NEW ZEALAND

Alexander Turnbull Library (National Library of New Zealand), 70 Molesworth Street, Wellington (Private Bag, Wellington) Auckland Institute and Museum Library, Auckland Domain (Private Bag, Auckland)

Auckland Public Library, cnr Wellesley & Lorne Streets, Auckland (PO Box 4138, Auckland)

Canterbury Museum Library, Rolleston Avenue, Christchurch

Canterbury Public Library, cnr Gloucester Street & Oxford Terrace, Christchurch (P.O. Box 1466, Christchurch)

Hamilton Public Library, 201 Alexandra Street,. Hamilton (PO Box 933, Hamilton)

Hocken Library, University of Otago, Castle Street, Dunedin (PO Box 56, Dunedin)

National Archives of New Zealand, Mulgrave Street, Wellington (PO Box 6148, Te Aro, Wellington)

National Library of New Zealand, 70 Molesworth Street, Wellington

National Archives Records Centre, B.J. Ball Bldg, Hardinge Street, (off Victoria Street West, Auckland (PO Box 2220, Auckland)

Registrar General, 1st Floor, 191 High Street, Lower Hutt (PO Box 31-115, Lower Hutt)

LDS Family History Centres:

Manurewa, Mt. Roskill; Takapuna; Christchurch; Dunedin; Gisborne; Hamilton; Temple View; Hastings; Invercargill; Kaikohe; Nelson; New Plymouth; Palmerston North; Rotorua; Upper Hutt; Wellington. (See telephone book under the Church of Jesus Christ of Latter-day Saints)

Family History Societies:

The New Zealand Society of Genealogists Inc., PO Box 8795, Auckland 3

Branches:

Alexandra: Mrs V. Loudon, 2 Glencarron Street, Alexandra

Auckland: Mrs Gwen Reiher, 1/29 Willcott Street, Auckland

Balclutha: June Stride, 107 Wilson Road, Balclutha

Blenheim: Mrs G. Burdon, 8 Watson Place, Blenheim

Canterbury: Mrs L. Bailey, 28 Hollis Avenue, Christchurch

Canterbury (mid): Mrs M. Cowan, 47 Thomson Street, Ashburton

Canterbury (sth): Mrs E. Jones, 39 Allnatt Street, Temuka

Dunedin: Mrs H. Bray, 26A Hargest Crescent, St Kilda

Feilding: Mrs Andrea Pickford, 4 Helena Place, Feilding

Gisborne: Mrs Isobel Coulston, 21 Emily Street, Gisborne

Gore: Doreen Hudson, Main South Road, No. 4 RD, Gore

Hamilton: C. Barbour, Willis Road, RD 10, Hamilton

Hauraki: Mrs S. Buchanan, Komaita, RD 4, Paeroa

Hawera: Y. Evans, 29 Erin Street, Hawera

Hawkes Bay: M. Murtagh, 904 Norrie Street, Hastings

Hibiscus Coast: Sue Gemmell, 32 Glenelg Road, Whangaparaoa

Howick: Sue Middleton, 54 Bramley Drive, Pakuranga

Huntly: Stephen Thwaites, 39 Kimihia Road, Huntly

Hutt Valley: Mrs Peggy Crawford, 59 Mabey Road, Lower Hutt

Kapiti: Mr Eric McNae, P.O. Box 48, Paraparaumu

Levin: D. Wenham, 7 Regal Street, Levin

Masterton: Joan Carter, 2 Fergusson Street, Masterton

Matamata: Joanna McKinnon, Box 318, Matamata

Morrinsville: Mrs H. Stone, Box 83, Morrinsville

Motueka: Mrs Coralie Smith, 41 Queen Victoria Street, Motueka

Nelson: Mrs C. MacKenzie, 183 Hampden Street, Nelson

New Plymouth: Mrs J. Bradley, 13 Kellyville Heights, New Plymouth

North Shore: Mrs G. Allison, 25 Juniper Road, Sunnynook, Auckland

Oamaru: Mr Don Allen, 7 Towey Street, Oamaru

Onehunga - Mrs Shirley Hinds, 11 Stavely Avenue, Hillsborough

Palmerston North - Suzanne Low, P.O. Box 1992, Palmerston North

Papakura: Iris Taylor, 63 Christmas Road, Manurewa

Papatoetoe: Marion Corles, 1/9 Hamilton Road, Papatoetoe

Pukekohe: Ross Miller, c/- Wesley College, P.O. Box 58, Pukekohe

Riccarton: Mr G. Dunbar, 19 Hadlow Place, Christchurch

Rotorua: Mrs Judy Andre, 71 Otonga Road, Rotorua

Southland: Mrs S. Ballinger, 150 Moana Street, Invercargill

Stratford: Mrs Carol Spragg, Mahoe Schoolhouse, RD 21, Stratford

Taihape: Kay Clark, 22 Pukeko Street, Taihape

Tauranga: Mrs Audrey Rosoman, 106 Mansel Road, Tauranga

Te Awamutu: Dick Crook, 193/1 Mutu Street, Awamutu

Te Kuiti: Mr Basil Kearton, 40 Hospital Road, Te Kuiti

Te Puke: Flora Gunn, Conway Road, c/- New Zealand Post, Paengaroa

Tokoroa: Mrs Iris Burt, 6 Dunkeld Place, Tokoroa

Waimate: Mrs Jean Stace, 4 Augustine Street, Waimate

Waitara: Mrs R. Sharman, 79 Mould Street, Waitara

Wanganui: Huia Kirk, 52 Wikitoria Road, Putiki

Warkworth: Cheryl Clague, 4 Mariners Grove, Algies Bay, Warkworth

Wellington: Yvonne Chisholm, 67B Horokiwi Road, Newlands, Wellington

Wellsford: Mrs L.J. Prictor, 3 RD, Wellsford

Whakatane: Mrs C. Violich, P.O. Box 2152, Kopeopeo

Whangamata: Mrs G. Staff, 223 Ocean Road, Whangamata

Whangarei: Jenny Clark, 4/205 Kiripaka Road, Whangarei

The New Zealand Family History Society Inc., P.O. Box 13, 301, Armagh, Christchurch.

Genealogy Terms

BDM — Births, Deaths and Marriages

Distaff — Female line. Your mother's line is equally as important as your father's line.

Family history — Finding out what people did, from birth to death.

Genealogy — The collecting of names, dates and places in the family tree.

IGI — The International Genealogical Index of over 200 million names worldwide, prepared by the Church of Jesus Christ of Latter-day Saints. It covers christenings and marriages from the 1500s to approximately 1880s, but is not complete.

Issue — Children

MI — Monumental Inscription or information recorded on a gravestone.

Microfiche/Microfilm — Most genealogical records have been reproduced on a microfiche or microfilm format. A microfiche is like a photograph compared to microfilm which is like a movie film on a role.

LDS — Nickname for The Church of Jesus Christ of Latter-day Saints. The Church houses the world's largest collection of genealogical records, copies of which can be hired through the various branches of the LDS Genealogical libraries.

Pedigree Chart — A chart showing your bloodline and lineage.

Siblings — Brothers and sisters.

Further Reading:

Books by Janet Reakes:

Census and Musters of Australia and the British Isles (Janet Reakes, 1992)

How to Trace Your Convict Ancestors (Hale & Iremonger, Sydney, 1989)
(Published as *The A to Z of Genealogy* by Mandarin, 1992)

How to Trace Your English Ancestors (Hale & Iremonger, Sydney, 1989)

How to Trace Your Family Tree and Not Get Stuck on a Branch (Hale & Iremonger, Sydney, 1992)

How to Trace Your Irish Ancestors (Hale & Iremonger, Sydney, 1992)

How to Trace Your Missing Ancestors, whether Living, Dead or Adopted (Hale & Iremonger, Sydney, 1986)

How to Trace Your Scottish Ancestors (Hale & Iremonger, Sydney, 1989)

How to Use the IGI and Wills (Janet Reakes, 1992)

Leaves on the Family Tree — How to Write the Family Story (Janet Reakes, 1986)

Overseas Research from Australia (Non British Countries) (Janet Reakes, 1992)

Professional Genealogists — How to Be One, How to Use One, How to Find One (Janet Reakes, 1986)

Shortcuts and Money Saving Ideas in Genealogy (Janet Reakes, 1992)

Tracing Family History in New Zealand by Anne Bromell (GP Books, Wellington, 1988)